EXTRAORDINARY DANGEROUS ANIMALS

Contents

D1530059

Animal Alert!

The animal world is a dangerous place! Angry rhinos charge through the grass, fierce lions stalk the plains, and deadly snakes lie in wait. One minute, animals are on the hunt for food, the next they're defending themselves from predators. A few animals attack people, but mainly they're out to get one another!

A Prickly Character

Size doesn't always win out in the animal kingdom. You might think a small porcupine is no match for a tough lion, but you'd be wrong. When a porcupine feels threatened, it raises the sharp quills on its back and tail. The young lion soon learns how sharp the jabbing spikes are, and it gives up!

Who Eats Whom?

Big animals usually eat small animals. Small animals, in turn, eat even smaller ones. The way that animals are linked together by what they eat — and what eats them — is called a food chain. Here's an example.

An anteater munches on tiny termites. It breaks into the termites' home with its sharp claws, then licks up the tasty insects with its super-long tongue.

But then the anteater ends up as dinner for a larger animal. A prowling jaguar jumps out of the bushes and pounces. It's the anteater who's the meal now!

A rhino charges to warn away attackers. You'd better get out of the way fast. Only an elephant is a match for this thick-skinned tank with a pointed horn twice as long as your arm!

3

Big and Bold

Here are a few animal heavyweights! One of the champions is the polar bear, the largest animal to roam the icy Arctic. A large animal such as this has few enemies. If another creature dares to approach, it is often knocked to the ground with a single blow!

Put 'Em Up!

When a polar bear stands up, it's almost twice as tall as you! Young polar bears love a good wrestling match. They hold onto each other with their thick paws, then roll around in the icy snow. They may even kick each other! But it's all in fun and teaches them how to defend themselves when they grow up.

TRUE STORY!

Eagles are big birds, which usually pick on fish or small mammals. But in 1932, in Norway, an eagle plucked a young girl from her yard. The kidnapper carried her in its talons to its nest high up on a mountain, but it dropped her on the way. Amazingly, the girl was found on a ledge, asleep and unharmed.

Most lizards are small, but not this one. The Komodo dragon is as long as a car! It catches animals as big as deer or wild pigs.

What

is so awesome about anacondas?

To start with, they're the heaviest snakes in the world. They grow to more than 30 feet (9 m) long, which is almost the length of a school bus!

An anaconda hugs other animals to death. It wraps itself around its victim. Then it squeezes hard — and suffocates it!

As a finishing touch, it gulps down its victim whole, then slinks off to rest. With a meal like that, it may not eat for another three months!

Small and Sinister

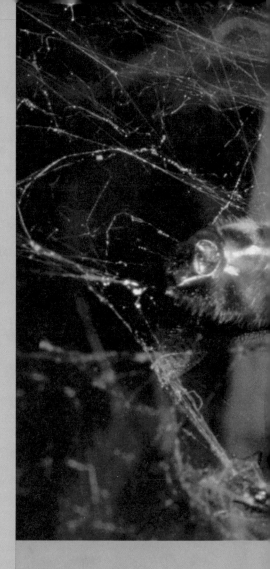

You don't have to be big to be dangerous. Many of the deadliest creatures on earth are also the tiniest. Being small has many advantages. For starters, it makes an animal tricky to spot so it can sneak up on its victim. It can also run off and hide if it comes under attack.

Meal for Two

Yummy! The female praying mantis has a habit of eating the male after mating. First, she bites off his head, then works her way down. But it's not quite as strange as it sounds. The male's body makes a healthy meal and helps to nourish the eggs that the female lays afterward.

Feet First?

A centipede spends the day under a log or a stone. But when night comes, it sets out to find dinner! Centipedes are famous for having lots of legs, but their first pair of legs isn't used for walking. Instead, these legs are used as fangs for injecting their unlucky prey, or victim, with poison.

A lethal male funnel web spider has captured a bee in its sticky web. This spider is so poisonous that its bite could kill a much bigger animal, such as a dog, in just a few hours.

Uh, oh!

That's Weird!

A black widow spider bites back if something, or someone, disturbs its web. Unfortunately, one of the places it likes to spin its web is in the bathroom!

BOO!

Team Tactics

Working together in a team means that animals such as wolves or lions can catch prey much bigger and stronger than they are. There is also safety in numbers. An attacker might take its chances against a lone wolf, but it's bound to think twice if a whole pack turns up.

EXTRA! EXTRA!
Wolves howl to tell one another what's happening. When a pack howls together, it sounds like there are many more wolves than there actually are. Scary!

When wolves go hunting, they follow a well-organized plan of attack. They set off in single file. When they spot a moose, they stand very still, then suddenly rush toward it.

Round 'Em Up

When killer whales are on the trail, the seas aren't safe! Their favorite dishes are fish, sharks, squid, and even dolphins and walruses. The whales may hunt in groups of up to 40 animals. They band together to round up fish and drive them to the shore where they can't escape. The fish are in a trap, ready to be snapped up!

In for the Kill

With needle-sharp teeth and snappy jaws, a school of tiny piranhas can strip a cow to the bone in minutes. Piranhas live in rivers in South America. They usually eat fruit, nuts, and other fish but if they are hungry and a bigger animal falls into the river, they'll attack at lightning speed.

Wow!

Huge armies of ants, several million strong, are on the march through South American rain forests. Any insects, spiders, or lizards that get in their way are soon outmaneuvered. In a regiment, army ants kill prey much more quickly and effectively than a lone operator.

Q. WHY DOES A WOLF CHEW GUM?   A. BECAUSE IT LIVES IN A PACK!

HA HA

Lions Rule!

Lions spend most of the day lounging around in the sun. But any passing gazelle or wildebeest had better watch out. When lions are hungry, they become aggressive. They use teamwork to stalk their prey, sneaking up on it by surprise. By the time their victim catches sight of the lions, it's too late.

Women's Work

In a lion's world, it's the females that do the work. When they spot a meal, they spread out in a line and begin to prowl. Slowly, they creep closer and closer, then, suddenly, one of them pounces. She knocks her victim to the ground, then bites its throat so that it suffocates. Female lions can kill animals as big as zebras or buffalo.

TRUE STORY!

Lions don't usually attack people. But in the 1800s, work on a railroad line in Africa had to be stopped because lions ate 135 workers!

Lions' Playschool

Learning is best when you're having fun! Lion cubs learn to hunt by pouncing on the end of their mother's tail and playing games of tag.

A male lion spends his day lazing around, but when dinner is served he grabs the best meat! He is bigger than the females, with a huge, furry mane to show who's in charge!

Claws and Paws

Powerful paws make deadly weapons for hunting. They are perfect for grabbing on to prey, and for scaring off enemies. And who needs a knife and fork for cutting up your food when you've got sharp, pointed claws?

A bear's claws are as long as your fingers! It uses its claws as fishhooks, to grab salmon from rivers. A bear also uses its paws as spades for digging up roots and small creatures.

Get a Grip

Take a look at a pet cat's paws. Now imagine them at least 10 times bigger — that's tiger-sized. A tiger can bring down its prey with a single bat of its paw. First, it grips with its long, sharp claws. Then, for a tighter hold, it pulls its claws in. Ouch!

That's Weird!

Thump! A cassowary is a bird with a mighty kick. This beastly bird can't fly, so its only defense is to kick box its way out of trouble. It has three dagger-sharp claws on each foot, which it uses to slash its enemies. It lives in the Australian rain forest.

What
do crabs use claws for?

Many crabs have big, blunt claws like hammers for smashing shellfish. Others use jagged claws like knives, to slice up their food.

Robber crabs live on land. They climb up coconut trees, then use their huge claws as nutcrackers to pry open the tasty coconuts.

Sea anemones are underwater animals with stinging tentacles. Boxer crabs grab a fistful of them and use them as boxing gloves to punch enemies!

Killers of the Night

When night falls, many animals head off to bed. But some creatures are just waking up, and they're ready for a midnight feast. These nighttime hunters have cunning ways of catching their food in the pitch dark. They don't miss a thing!

  A temple viper spots a nighttime snack using a clever secret weapon. This sneaky snake has two tiny holes on either side of its head, which sense the heat given off by an animal's body.

Nose Nibblers

Vampire bats sneak up on sleeping animals and nip their skin with their razor-sharp fangs. Then they slurp up their blood! These greedy guzzlers slurp about a tablespoon of blood a day. Vampire bats live in Central and South America and usually feed on cows and horses. But occasionally they snack on human fingers, noses, and toes!

Ghosts in the Night

Is it a ghost? Is it a plane? No, it's a barn owl on the lookout for food. Barn owls use finely tuned hearing and supersharp eyesight to track mice. They glide along, then swoop down silently to grab their victims with their spiky talons.

EXTRA! EXTRA!

The temple viper took its name from the Snake Temple in Penang, Malaysia, which is crawling with these creatures! They are thought to bring good luck!

That's Weird!

The spine-chilling story of Dracula was based on the behavior of real-life vampire bats. According to legend, Dracula was an evil human who turned into a vampire at night. Then he set off to find victims to suck their blood.

Dinner tonight??

Teeth and Fangs

If a crocodile grins at you, run for your life! It's probably eyeing you as its dinner. All those sharp teeth in the crocodile's big mouth are weapons for snapping up prey. Other animals have frightful fangs for injecting their prey with deadly poison. You have been warned!

Wow!

A hippo might look big and cuddly — until you pick a fight. Its huge lower teeth are as long as your arm! Male hippos fight to protect their territory. They open their mouths wide and lunge at each other with their great big choppers!

This Won't Hurt

A rattlesnake's fangs are like two pointed tubes filled with poison. Usually, they are folded back against the roof of its mouth. But when the snake strikes, its fangs swing into a biting position, ready to sink in!

Who's

got the oddest choppers?

A male narwhal has a huge tooth that grows into a spiral more than 6.5 feet (2 m) long. He uses it for jousting with other males!

Walrus tusks are really teeth that grow up to 3.25 feet (1 m) long. The walrus uses these to haul itself over the ice and to stab enemies.

A sawfish has a long, flat snout, lined with 20 pairs of teeth. The sawfish swims into a school of fish and slashes this saw from side to side to kill them.

A crocodile can leap right out of the water to grab its prey. Then it spins around to tear off chunks of meat!

Poison Power!

What do animals such as snakes, frogs, and scorpions have in common? Some of them are poisonous, that's what! They use killer poisons to finish off their prey and to frighten enemies. But they all have different ways of delivering their deadly venom, so watch out!

EXTRA! EXTRA!
Poison dart frogs can be really tiny. This one reaches a maximum length of only 0.9 inches (18 mm)!

The poison dart frog's colorful skin tells enemies to stay away! Rain forest people roast the frogs to release their poison. Then they dip the tips of their hunting arrows into this poison.

It's a Sting Thing!

A scorpion's tail is a deadly weapon. If the scorpion is under attack or hunting for dinner, it grabs its victim with its huge front claws. Then it curls its tail over its head and strikes with perfect accuracy, paralyzing the victim. This gecko is in big trouble!

Surprise Tactic

1 More than 2,000 years ago, a general named Hannibal fought the Romans in a battle at sea. He badly needed a winning tactic...

2 ...so legend has it that he ordered his men to throw jars of live poisonous snakes into the Roman ships. Amazingly enough, he won the battle!

Champion Spitter

When a cobra is angry, a hood at the back of its neck flares up in warning. One type of cobra, when it's really mad, spits poison into its enemy's eyes. The spitting cobra can hit its target from about 6.5 feet (2 m) away!

Underwater Terrors!

The ocean is a strange, dark, and hazardous place. Millions of amazing sea creatures are out to get one another, using bizarre weapons and tactics! It's a fish-eat-fish world down there....

Killer Cones

If you think seashells are pretty harmless, think again! A cone shell is a venomous creature. If disturbed, it shoots out a harpoonlike tooth, which hooks into the unsuspecting victim. The cone shell then injects a poison strong enough to paralyze a fish, snail, or worm.

Sinister Stones

The deadliest fish in the sea is also one of the strangest. It sits on the seabed, posing as a rock, waiting for a passing meal. It's well disguised, so it can't be seen until it's too late. The stonefish then stabs its victim with poisonous spines, which are sharp enough to pierce a rubber-soled shoe.

TRUE STORY!

In olden days, sailors were terrified by tales of a nightmarish sea monster known as a kraken. Said to look like a cross between an octopus and a squid, the kraken could easily tip over a ship. The legend is probably based on the harmless real-life giant squid, which has tentacles 15 times as long as your legs.

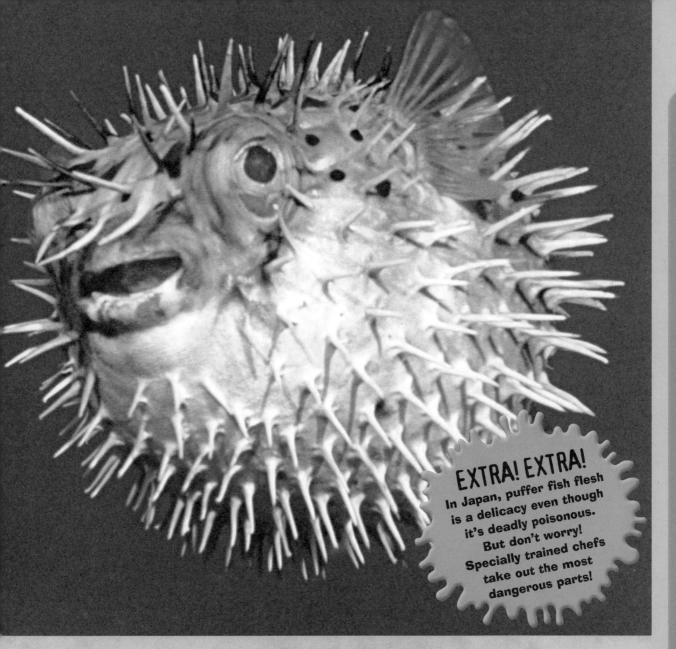

EXTRA! EXTRA!
In Japan, puffer fish flesh is a delicacy even though it's deadly poisonous. But don't worry! Specially trained chefs take out the most dangerous parts!

If an enemy nibbles at a puffer fish, it's in for a big surprise. The puffer fish swallows water or air and blows itself up to the size of a basketball to stop itself from being eaten!

Shock! Horror!

Touch an electric eel and you're in for a nasty shock. These slippery river fish zap their prey with electricity. The electricity is made in the muscles and nerves in the eel's long tail. One shock is enough to kill a fish, or even stun a human.

You'll fry tonight!

HA HA

21

Shark Attack!

There's a danger lurking deep in the sea. With its telltale pointed fin and massive jaws, it's a fearsome killer. And it can strike at anytime. You won't even hear it coming. Just when you thought it was safe to go into the water, here comes a hungry shark!

EXTRA! EXTRA!
A great white shark has thousands of terrible teeth, arranged in rows. When one row wears out, another simply slides into place!

If a great white shark senses blood, it goes hunting. It aims for its prey at top speed, then opens its mouth and bites hard. Luckily, this one's just biting on a buoy!

Swimming with Sharks

A few brave scientists go swimming with sharks for fun. They work inside metal cages or wear shark-proof suits. The suits are made from tiny, linked metal rings that even a sharp-toothed shark can't bite through. Wearing a striped swimsuit is another way of avoiding attack. The shark thinks the person's a poisonous sea snake and avoids him or her.

TRUE STORY!

Even dead sharks can bite! In the 1970s, a fisherman in Australia was involved in a car crash. He was thrown onto the back seat of the car where a set of shark's jaws was lying. The unlucky driver needed 22 stitches in his wounds.

Maybe we need a dentist?

Do sharks really eat people?

Hello!

Yikes!

There are about 375 different types of sharks. Most of them are fairly shy and would be more scared of you than you are of them!

Sharks don't normally eat people, but sometimes they make mistakes. From a shark's point of view, a surfer looks a lot like a seal!

Please be nice to me!

People have hunted some types of sharks, such as the great white, so there aren't many left. In some countries, laws exist to protect sharks.

Watch Out!

It's surprising, but the animals that pose the biggest threat to humans aren't sharks or rhinos. Instead, they're tiny insects. These minute monsters can spread diseases or destroy whole fields of crops!

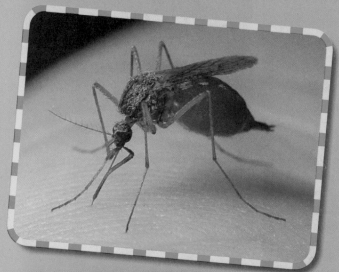

Tiny Biters!

Tiny mosquitoes are dangerous because they can spread a disease called malaria. First, the female mosquito bites you and sucks your blood. Then it spits tiny creatures, called parasites, into you. Parasites live off you and make you sick. People with malaria suffer from sweating, fever, and headaches. They need a doctor right away!

What Was the Black Plague?

1 The Black Plague was a terrible disease that wiped out 25 million people in Europe and Asia in the 1300s. It was spread by bloodsucking fleas that lived on black rats!

Mmm, dinner!

2 Rats were everywhere. If their fleas bit anyone, that person would get the disease. Most victims died within a few days. Doctors in those days couldn't do much to help!

Wow!

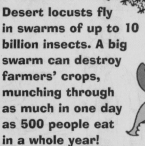

Desert locusts fly in swarms of up to 10 billion insects. A big swarm can destroy farmers' crops, munching through as much in one day as 500 people eat in a whole year!

EXTRA! EXTRA!
This tsetse fly looks like a huge monster, but it's really only 0.2 inches (4 mm) long. It's shown about 70 times larger than its true size.

Q. WHAT did THE TWO LOCUSTS SAY TO THE FLEA?   A. FLEA'S A CROWD!

HA HA

In Africa, the tsetse fly is a real danger. It sucks people's blood and infects people with a killer disease called sleeping sickness, which makes the sufferer feel achy and sleepy.

Ancient Hunters

Millions of years ago, the world was a very different place. Animals that roamed the earth back then no longer exist today. Among the fiercest were meat-eating dinosaurs. You'd be out of luck if you were a mild-mannered plant eater, happily munching on leaves!

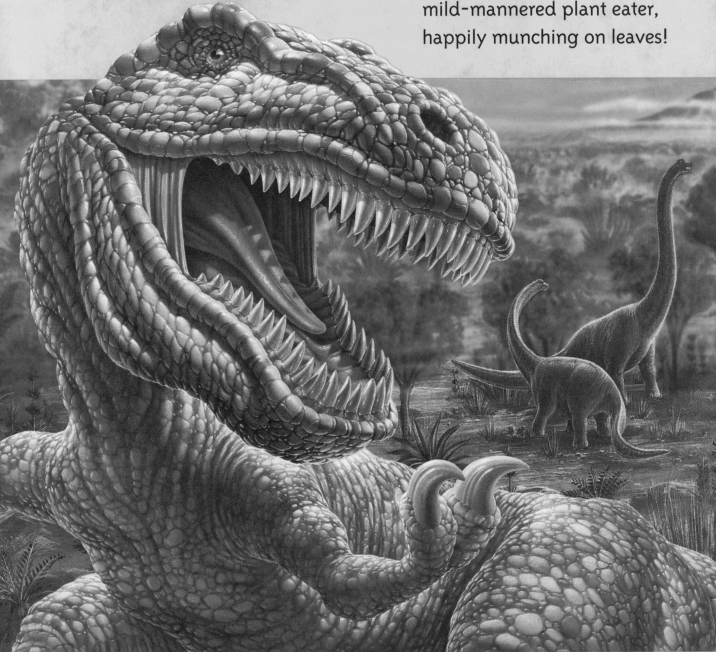

Terrifying *Tyrannosaurus rex* was a massive meat-eating dinosaur. It had a huge head and superstrong jaws lined with big, scary teeth like long, sharp steak knives.

About 11 million years ago, a huge cat called *Smilodon* roamed the grasslands and woodlands of North and South America. But it wasn't likely to lap up a saucer of milk. It was the size of a leopard, and its enormous, stabbing fangs were almost as long as a page in this book.

Speedy Slasher

Velociraptor was a lightweight, fast-moving dinosaur that sprinted along on two legs. It had two long, grabbing arms to snatch its prey and a sickle-shaped claw on each of its feet to slash and tear at its victims.

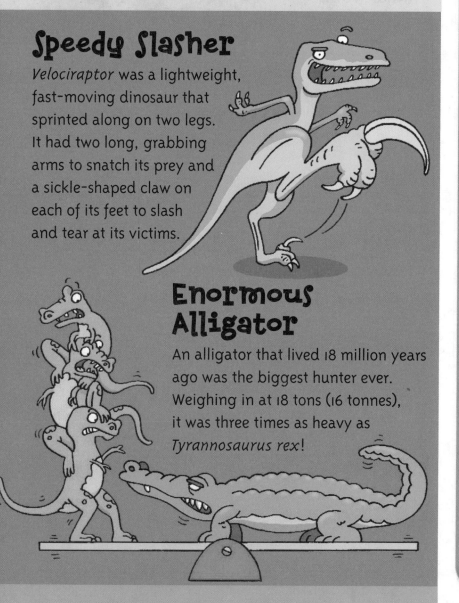

Enormous Alligator

An alligator that lived 18 million years ago was the biggest hunter ever. Weighing in at 18 tons (16 tonnes), it was three times as heavy as *Tyrannosaurus rex*!

Which

dinosaurs were armed?

Stegosaurus was a plant eater. It defended itself with a spiky tail, which was perfect for taking a huge swipe at enemies.

Triceratops was another plant eater. It was built like a rhinoceros with huge horns nearly 3.25 feet (1 m) long. It used these to stab attackers.

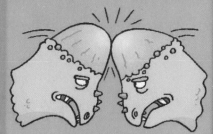

Pachycephalosaurus had a thick, bony skull, which worked as a helmet in head-butting battles. This is how it got its nickname "bonehead"!

27

Extra Amazing

Who are the top terrors of the animal world? Which are the fastest, the mightiest, and the most poisonous? Here are a few animals that deserve a place in the extra-dangerous record book!

Gruesome Gripper

Only four types of mammals are poisonous, and the deadliest of these is the platypus. A male platypus has stinging spurs on its ankles. It can kill animals as big as dogs in its ghastly grip. Mostly, though, it uses its spurs when it's fighting another platypus.

Draw on the count of three!

Way to Go, Mako

The fastest shark is the mako. No one's sure of its top speed, but people think it can zoom through the water at up to 60 miles per hour (96 kmh) — as fast as a car on the open road. It is superstrong and is one of the fastest fish of all.

Sprint Star

Don't bother trying to outrun a cheetah. You'll soon run out of steam, because it's the fastest animal on land! When a cheetah is chasing its prey, it can race along at about 65 miles per hour (104 kmh). Its sharp claws grip the ground as it runs, like the spikes on a sprinter's running shoes. The cheetah uses its long tail to balance, keeping it straight on target.

Fangs a Lot

The gabon viper from Africa has the longest snake fangs of all. They're 2.5 inches (6.35 cm) long — that's as long as your finger. They could pierce you to the bone!

Sneaky Spider

Don't make friends with a Brazilian wandering spider — it's one of the world's most poisonous spiders. It's particularly nasty for humans because it likes to sneak inside homes and hide in clothes and shoes. So watch your step!

It's Got Clout

Most bears are strong and bulky, but the heaviest hitter is the Alaskan brown bear. It can weigh a mighty 1,650 pounds (750 kg) — the weight of a small car. But for such a large animal, it's surprisingly agile. If it takes a swipe at an enemy, it would be an instant knockout.

True or False?

Are you an animal expert? Test your knowledge and say whether you think these statements are true or false. Answers are on page 32, but no cheating!

1. A cassowary is a champion kick boxer.
2. A great white shark has 300 teeth.
3. A wolf hunts on its own.
4. A puffer fish blows at its enemies until they go away.
5. This animal's favorite food is riverbank plants.

6. A mosquito is not at all dangerous.

Animal Terms

fangs
Long teeth that animals use to bite or poison prey.

fin
A fold of bony skin on a fish's body. A fish uses its fin to steer through the water.

food chain
The way living things are linked together by what they eat. Big animals usually eat smaller animals which, in turn, eat smaller animals and plants.

malaria
A deadly disease that is spread by mosquitoes. It gives you a fever and can even kill you.

mammal
An animal that feeds its babies milk and cares for them after they are born. Mammals include shrews, kangaroos, elephants, and humans.

narwhal
A type of whale that lives in the Arctic Ocean.

pack
A group of animals, such as wolves, that lives and hunts together.

paralyze
To injure a human or animal so that it can't move.

7. A rhino's horn is longer than your arm.

8. Lion cubs play tag.

9. A vampire bat eats fruit and leaves.

10. The temple viper is said to be lucky.

11. The anaconda is the world's shortest snake.

12. The animal in this picture is the fastest runner on land.

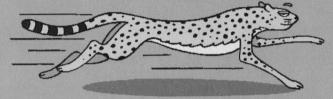

13. A bear uses its claws as fishhooks to catch salmon.

14. Armies of ants have several million soldiers.

15. A cobra can spit at its enemies.

16. One kind of fish can look like a stone.

17. A tiger's claws are the same size as a house cat's.

18. *Tyrannosaurus rex* was only a plant-eating dinosaur.

19. A black widow spider can live indoors.

20. This frog couldn't hurt anything.

parasite
A plant or animal that lives and feeds off another animal or plant.

poison
A substance that causes damage or death to living things if it gets inside the body.

predator
An animal that hunts and eats other animals.

prey
An animal that is hunted and eaten by other animals.

pride
A group of lions that lives together. It consists of an adult male, several females, and their young.

rain forest
A thick forest that grows in hot regions of the world, such as in some areas of South America.

school
A group of fish or other animals that lives together underwater.

talons
Long, sharp claws on the feet of birds, such as eagles.

tusk
A long, curved, pointed tooth sticking out from the mouth of an animal, such as a walrus.

venomous
Another word for poisonous.

Index

Answers

1	True	11	False
2	False	12	True
3	False	13	True
4	False	14	True
5	False	15	True
6	False	16	True
7	True	17	False
8	True	18	False
9	False	19	True
10	True	20	False

Author: Anita Ganeri
Illustrations: Andrew Peters; p. 26 Adrian Chesterman.
Consultant: Barbara Taylor, BSc
Photographs: Cover: Bruce Coleman Inc.; p. 2 Tony Stone Images;
p. 3 NHPA/John Shaw; p. 4 Tony Stone Images; p. 5 Ardea London/Adrian
Warren; p. 6 Ardea London/Hans Dossenbach; pp. 6-7 Scott Camazine/Oxford
Scientific Films; pp. 8-9 Jeff Lepore/Science Photo Library; p. 10 NHPA/Andy
Rouse; p. 11 Tom McHugh/Science Photo Library; p. 12 Ardea/M. Watson;
p. 13 George Holton/Science Photo Library; pp. 14-15 David T. Roberts/Nature's
Images/Science Photo Library; p. 15 Michael & Patricia Fogden/CORBIS;
p. 16 Tom McHugh/ Science Photo Library; p. 17 Jeff Rotman/BBC Natural
History Unit; p. 18 Tim Davis/Science Photo Library; p. 19 NHPA/Daniel
Heuclin; p. 20 Rudiger Lehnen/Science Photo Library; p. 21 J.W. Mowbray
/Science Photo Library; pp. 22-23 NHPA/Mark Bowler; p. 23 Jeff Rotman/BBC
Natural History Unit; p. 24 Ardea/Steve Hopkins; p. 25 Eye of Science/Science
Photo Library; pp. 28-29 NHPA/Nigel J. Dennis.

Created by **act-two** for Scholastic Inc. Copyright © **act-two**, 2001
All rights reserved. Published by Scholastic Inc.

SCHOLASTIC and associated logos are trademarks and/or registered
trademarks of Scholastic Inc.

ISBN 0-439-28320-5

12 11 10 9 8 7 6   4 5 6/0

Printed in the U.S.A.

First Scholastic printing, September 2001